From Flower to Fruit

From Flower to Fruit

Richard Konicek-Moran

Kathleen Konicek-Moran

NSTA Kids

National Science Teachers Association

Arlington, Virginia

National Science Teachers Association

Claire Reinburg, Director
Wendy Rubin, Managing Editor
Rachel Ledbetter, Associate Editor
Donna Yudkin, Book Acquisitions Coordinator

ART AND DESIGN
Will Thomas Jr., Director
Himabindu Bichali, Cover, Interior Design
Original illustrations by Kathleen Konicek-Moran

PRINTING AND PRODUCTION
Catherine Lorrain, Director

NATIONAL SCIENCE TEACHERS ASSOCIATION
David L. Evans, Executive Director
David Beacom, Publisher

1840 Wilson Blvd., Arlington, VA 22201
www.nsta.org/store
For customer service inquiries, please call 800-277-5300.

Lexile® measure: 910L

Library of Congress Cataloging-in-Publication Data
Names: Konicek-Moran, Richard, author. | Konicek-Moran, Kathleen, author, illustrator.
Title: From flower to fruit / by Richard and Kathleen Konicek-Moran; illustrated by Kathleen Konicek-Moran.
Description: Arlington, VA : National Science Teachers Association, [2016] | Audience: K to grade 3.
Identifiers: LCCN 2016023439 | ISBN 9781941316344 (book)
Subjects: LCSH: Plant anatomy--Juvenile literature. | Plants--Reproduction--Juvenile literature. | Flowers--Juvenile literature. | Fruit--Juvenile literature.
Classification: LCC QK641 .K6727 2016 | DDC 581--dc23 LC record available at https://lccn.loc.gov/2016023439

e-ISBN: 978-1-941316-36-8

About This Book

The purpose of *From Flower to Fruit* is to inspire young children to appreciate the wonder of nature—specifically, the flowers that bloom throughout the growing season—and understand the importance of flowers in every ecosystem. Adults can read this book to younger children, or older children can read the book individually as an activity. More than just a pretty book, *From Flower to Fruit* is intended to create an interest in and curiosity about flowers so that children will look carefully at them and their fruits. The goals of this book support the biology practices, core ideas, and concepts outlined in the *Next Generation Science Standards* (NGSS Lead States 2013).

The book illustrates the daylily *(Hemerocallis sp.)* and the balloon flower *(Platycodon grandiflorus)* because they are large "perfect" flowers, meaning they have both male and female parts that are obvious to even the casual observer. Of course, not all flowers are so easily observed, and not all flowers are perfect. For example, in the dandelion *(Taraxacum officinale)*, each tiny petal is a complete flower. On the shrubs of the holly *(Ilex sp.)*, male and female flowers are located on separate plants.

For children, finding the reproductive parts of flowers in their environment can turn into an investigation once children are able to recognize the basic differences between parts. Adults who are guiding the investigations can use the brief background on flower and fruit anatomy at the end of the book as a reference. Flowers can provide great teaching and learning opportunities for all ages. Botany, the study of plants, has been grossly underrated as a topic for investigation, perhaps because botany is commonly considered more of a memorizing or categorizing science. We hope this book will introduce the discovery and wonder of botany.

Plants have evolved over the years to provide some of the most amazing structures in the biological world: flowers and fruits featured in this book, internal vessels that defy gravity as they transport food and water, and roots that respond to touch. Moreover, plants have developed methods of modifying their structures and chemicals to repel predators and are essential to the incredible chemical reaction of photosynthesis. Plants make up 99% of the biomass in our biosphere, so they are difficult to ignore. They provide us with food, nutrition, and oxygen for our respiration. Plants also remove potentially dangerous chemicals such as carbon dioxide from our atmosphere.

On the macro level, plants provide food for smaller creatures such as our beloved butterflies and honeybees, not to mention moths, beetles, hummingbirds, and bats. They also provide adornment for homes and dresses. Plants are near the bottom of the food chain, and without plants, no animals, including humans, could live. On an economic level, plants provide lumber and resources that are important to our world economy—oil and natural gas (giving whales a break from being the only source of lubricants and fuel for hundreds of years).

Although the book's botanical investigations may have limitations, especially for children in urban environments who may not have many flowers outside to observe, we urge you to try to find opportunities for children to examine real flowers. They can be purchased quite inexpensively at the supermarket and brought back to the home or classroom. Be aware, however, of the types of flowers you buy. Perfect flowers such as those portrayed in this book are hard to find. Most of the flowers in supermarkets are what are known as *composite* flowers—for example, mums and carnations. Composite flowers, such as the dandelion, have many hundreds of flowers in their heads and are difficult to examine for parts, but they are interesting to examine if you have a microscope available. Fruits, however, are more readily available and fun to look into and break down into carpel and seeds. As you work with flowers, remember that some children may be allergic to them or to insects found on them. Make sure medical conditions are known before conducting investigations. The "Activities" section (p. 32) provides additional safety guidelines that should be adopted and enforced to create a safer learning experience for each child.

It is important for children to have their own magnifier as they view plants. The magnifier does not have to be expensive; small plastic magnifiers do a great job. It is also important that children use the magnifier correctly. Bringing the lens to the eye and then down to the subject at a length that will bring the subject into focus will yield the best result. Each plant that children look at or dissect will bring questions that can lead to further investigation. As the parent or teacher, you should join in the spirit of discovery and investigate plants that are new to you as well so that you can demonstrate exploration. As you and young scientists look through a lens or dissect a flower, interesting topics will come up to discuss, research on the internet or in botany books, and share together.

Reference

NGSS Lead States. 2013. *Next Generation Science Standards: For states, by states*. Washington, DC: National Academies Press. *www.nextgenscience.org/next-generation-science-standards*.

Imagine that you have some friends in your neighborhood whom you know really well. You call them Mr. Ty (his real name is Tyrone) and Mrs. Maria. They used to be teachers. You like to help them in their garden, which always seems to be in bloom. One day, you help them clean out their attic. The attic is filled with lots of boxes and trunks and old toys from their children who have grown up and moved away from home. You discover a magnifying glass that Mrs. Maria said she thought she had lost.

"Do you want it?" she asks.

She shows you some of the pictures of plants she drew when she was younger. She was a botanical artist before becoming a teacher.

"When you draw something, you look very closely at it and see things you might have missed if you were not drawing it," Mrs. Maria tells you.

"Awesome!" you say. Holding your new tool, you turn to Mr. Ty and ask, "Can you help me use the magnifying glass? Maybe I can draw some pictures too."

"Well, sure!" Mr. Ty says. "With a magnifying glass, we can see things we couldn't see without it. Be sure to hold it up to your eye and bend down to bring it close to what you want to see. Let's go out in the garden and see what we can study. Bunnies and birds move around too much, so I guess that leaves us with plants to look at. Good thing, too, because observing plants lets you see some pretty cool things!"

In the garden, you see a big, beautiful lily and bring your face and the glass down until the inner part of the flower suddenly becomes clear. To your amazement, you see a lot of what look like tiny sticks coming out of the middle of the flower.

"What are those?" you ask, pointing to them.

"Those are special parts of the flower," Mr. Ty answers. "Look closely at them and tell me what you see. Are they all the same?"

As you look, you see that they aren't all the same. Some have gold-colored dust on their tips. One is longer than the others and does not have any dust on it.

The magnifying glass gives you a "bee's-eye view" of what is in the flower. In fact, as you look at the flower, you see a bee deep inside.

"Why does the bee go so far inside the flower?" you ask.

Mrs. Maria says the bee is searching for nectar—the sweet stuff that some plants make deep in their petals. Butterflies, moths, hummingbirds, beetles, and bees love to take this nutritious food back to their young or just eat it to keep their energy going. She tells you that bees are very important to the world because of what this bee is doing right now!

You see the bee bump the bunch of stalks topped
with that gold dust that Mr. Ty says is called pollen.

Mr. Ty says that the stalk with the pollen on it is called a stamen, and when the bee bumps it, down comes the pollen like a snowstorm. You can see that the pollen sticks to the bee's back and legs.

He adds, "You can usually tell which of the sticklike things are the stamens because of the golden pollen on them, but there is another special part that can be different in each flower."

Suddenly, the bee spreads its wings. "Watch that bee!" shouts Mr. Ty.

The bee heads off to the next flower and carries the pollen with it. As the bee searches roughly for the nectar in the next flower, some of the pollen comes off its body and sticks to the end of the tall stalk in the center of the flower. That flower part looks like it has a sticky goo on top, and Mrs. Maria calls that part the pistil.

"Why do you think it is sticky?" asks Mrs. Maria.

"It's sticky so that when the pollen lands on it, the pollen doesn't fall off," you answer.

"That makes a lot of sense, doesn't it?" says Mrs. Maria.

Mrs. Maria says that scientists who study plants use even stronger magnifying lenses, and they have found that pollen has special cells in it that are necessary to form seeds and fruits. She also explains that all living things are made of cells—the building blocks of life.

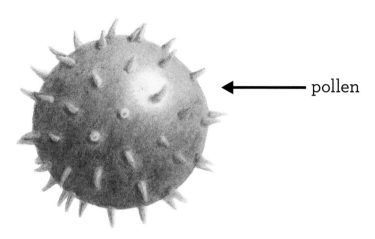

pollen

Mrs. Maria says that one cell in the pollen forms a tube that goes down the pistil stalk until it reaches a different cell called an egg, which is inside an ovary.

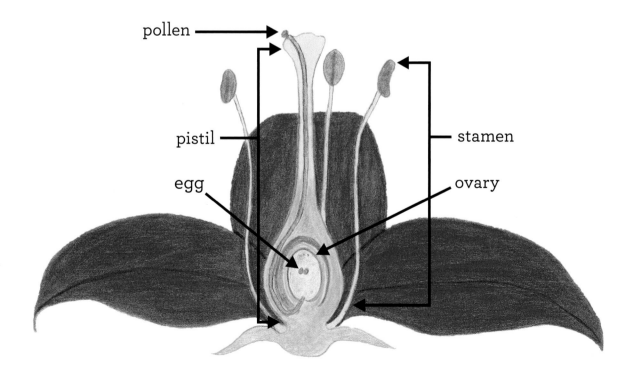

pollen

pistil

egg

stamen

ovary

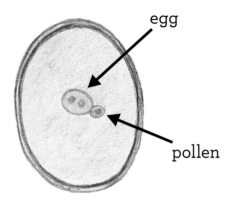

egg

pollen

Another cell from the pollen slides down the tube and combines with the egg. This is the beginning of the seed.

The tissue around the seed—the ovary—then grows thicker and forms a fruit that protects the seed. Mrs. Maria draws you some pictures to help you understand.

Mr. Ty picks a green bean from the garden and slices one of its seeds in half with his thumb. Inside, you can see the beginnings of a tiny plant with your magnifying glass.

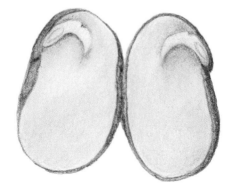

"The seed is a baby plant. As it grows in the fruit, the seed contains everything it needs to form a new plant," explains Mrs. Maria. "As the seed grows, so does the ovary. Together, they form a fruit."

Mr. Ty shows you the daylily fruit and uses scissors to open the fruit down the middle. You see lots of seeds inside. Then, he breaks one crosswise so you can see the inside of the fruit from another angle.

"Are all fruits like this?" you ask.

"Well, you eat fruit almost every day," says Mrs. Maria. "Do they all look like this?"

"You mean fruits like melons and plums and blueberries?"

"Yes," says Mr. Ty. "And tomatoes and zucchini, too, but we don't put them in a fruit salad."

"Tomatoes and zucchini!" you exclaim, laughing. "They're not fruits, they're vegetables!"

Mr. Ty explains that scientists consider any vegetable that has seeds in it a fruit. Some of our vegetables do not have seeds, such as celery, sweet potatoes, and carrots. However, many foods that chefs call vegetables scientists would consider fruits.

"Do all fruits get eaten?" you ask.

"Well, some animal usually eats them. Remember how my dogs used to eat the raspberries right off the bushes? But there are other fruits—such as the parachute-like fruits on the dandelion flower—that grow on trees, bushes, or weeds that aren't all that tasty, even to animals," Mrs. Maria explains. "And some fruits are made to travel—by flying in the air, floating on the water, or sticking to your socks! You wouldn't believe all the different forms fruit takes."

"Did you say that trees have fruit?" you ask. "Are trees plants?"

"They certainly are. Trees grow using the Sun and water, and they have green parts like these daylilies here. You have eaten lots of fruit from trees—apples and oranges, right? And don't forget acorns from oak trees, which squirrels love. They are fruits too."

"Some fruits land in a good spot to grow," says Mr. Ty. "Let's say you throw away an apple core or a peach pit in the garden and it sprouts and grows. Or say a squirrel forgets to dig up an acorn and up comes an oak tree. Or maybe"—he gives you a big smile—"we'll just plant one of these bean seeds and see what comes up."

Mr. Ty puts a green bean seed in a clear plastic cup with holes in it. Then, he adds some soil and water to the cup.

"Now you can see how the seed grows!" he says.

Over the next eight weeks, you keep visiting Mr. Ty and Mrs. Maria's garden and observe the green bean seed's growth. First, you see roots grow from the bottom of the seed. Then, you see one little leaf, which later turns into two leaves.

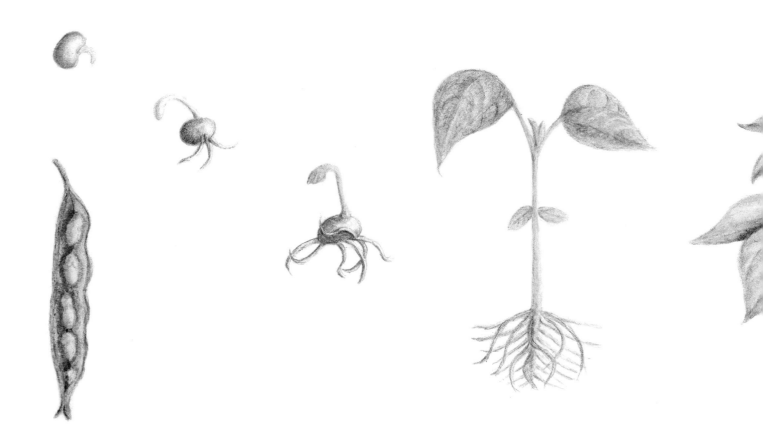

After Mr. Ty plants the growing seed in the ground, lots of leaves that are in threes start to sprout. Then, beautiful flowers appear. Finally, you see beans! Mr. Ty reminds you that beans are the fruit of the plant.

One day, you're in their garden examining flowers with your magnifying glass again.

Mrs. Maria says, "You can look for other flowers to see if you can see their flower parts."

She points to some blue flowers in the garden and tells you they are called balloon flowers. You look at one of them with your magnifying lens. You wonder, "Can I tell the stamens from the pistils?"

You look around the garden and find other flowers that you can observe closely through the lens. You discover that you can usually tell which parts are the stamens because of their gold or brown pollen, but the pistils of the different flowers often look very different

"It's getting warm. How about a nice cool glass of lemonade?" says Mrs. Maria. "Let's go into the kitchen and look at all of the fruits we have."

Mrs. Maria, Mr. Ty, and you leave the garden and head inside. On the kitchen table are many kinds of fruits, and you see how different they are. Yet they all came from flowers. Amazing, huh?

Activities

1. Different kinds of flowers exist that do not look like the ones illustrated in the story. Balloon flowers are similar to daylilies, but dandelions and sunflowers are different from balloon flowers. See if you can find the parts in balloon flowers, dandelions, and sunflowers as well. You may have to take the flower apart to do this activity. (*Safety note:* Always wash your hands after handling plants. If observing flowers in the wild, avoid contact with harmful plants such as poison ivy, poison oak, and poison sumac.)

2. Try to germinate some of the seeds you find in fruit. Put them in a clear plastic bag with some wet paper towels and observe them daily. Draw the changes as you see them. (*Safety note:* Be aware that mold may grow in the bag. Some children are allergic to mold, so remind everyone not to open the bags.)

3. Try to draw a flower, and be really careful to draw exactly what you see.

4. Seeds travel from place to place. See if you can find out how different seeds move around. You might collect various seeds and look at them through a magnifying glass. (*Safety note:* Use caution when bringing objects near the eye to prevent injury.)

5. Find a flowering berry plant such as a blueberry, raspberry, strawberry, or even a maple tree. Watch the fruit develop over time and draw the different stages of growth. How does the flower change as the fruit ripens?

6. What would happen to a plant without a pistil? Cut off the pistil of a growing flower with scissors and see if the flower bears fruit. Draw what happens. (*Safety note:* Always wash your hands after handling plants.)

Background Information for Parents and Teachers

About 250 million years ago, something marvelous happened. Up to that point, large plants mostly relied on the wind to carry pollen from one plant to another, and new seeds formed during fertilization were unprotected and could be easily destroyed by many forces. Examples of these plants are still around and known as *conifers* (e.g., pines, hemlocks, and firs). Conifers are *gymnosperms,* which means naked seeds. Later, flowering plants emerged. Scientists don't exactly know how these flowering plants came to be, but they do know that their occurrence changed everything. The flowers produced fruits that protected the seeds! Flowering plants are called *angiosperms,* and their seeds are enclosed in a structure called an *ovary,* which ultimately turns into fruit. The new plants-to-be were protected, and the fruits were often so delicious that animals found them wonderful to eat. Many plants evolved to allow their seeds to pass right through the intestines of animals and fall to the ground surrounded by natural "fertilizer."

Enclosed seeds resulted from changes in the development of the ovary. In time, the ovary expanded in a multitude of ways, resulting in many means of seed dispersal. These methods of dispersing seeds include wind (e.g., tiny seeds are caught by air currents, and incredibly engineered parachute and helicopter seed forms, such as those of dandelions and maple seeds, ride on breezes); water; and, of course, animals (both by ingestion and by developing seed forms that easily "hitch a ride" as cockle-burs do). All of these methods not only help the plant reproduce itself but also land the baby plants far away from the parent, where there is less competition for light and other resources.

There are many kinds of fruits. One major misconception common in adults and children is the belief that many of the vegetables we eat are technically fruits. A *fruit* is defined as any seed-bearing structure that develops from a flower. Vegetables can be leaves (lettuce), stalks (celery), roots (potatoes), or flower buds (broccoli). Botanists and chefs have different opinions about what is a vegetable and what is a fruit. As Mr. Ty said, "Tomatoes and zucchini ... [are fruits], but we don't put them in a fruit salad."

With the development of angiosperms came a switch from just wind pollination to a more complicated form of pollination involving an animal facilitator (known as a *pollinator*). Beetles were among the first insects to help pollinate the earliest flowers. About 85 million years later, bees, wasps, butterflies, moths, birds, and bats evolved to participate in the insect–flower relationship. The transfer of pollen and the subsequent fertilization were no longer such hit-or-miss operations as they had been for the gymnosperms. Rather, the process developed into a quite complicated dance that involved scent and nectar production and incredible coloration of flower petals.

Botanists classify fruits into many different categories (e.g., samara, capsule, drupe), but these distinctions may be too much information for most children in lower grade levels. The most common forms of fruits are depicted on pages 20–23, so you can refer to those images if older children are interested in learning more about the various categories. You can find an excellent presentation about fruit classification at *www.slideshare.net/karthisivasamy/types-of-fruits-23636429?next_slideshow=1.*

As we have noted in previous publications (see the *Everyday Science Mysteries* series published by the National Science Teachers Association), children—and even adults—hold comparatively incomplete ideas about their observations of natural phenomena. They develop these incomplete ideas to try to explain what they see. Educators call them preconceptions, although they are sometimes called misconceptions. We prefer *preconception,* because *mis*conception has a pejorative connotation and *pre*conception adequately implies a place that everyone starts from when trying to bring naïve ideas closer to the ones modern scientists believe to be true. Because these preconceptions have often been held for a long time, they are difficult to change. Educators should try to understand children's preconceptions and build bridges to help them grasp more comprehensive explanations for natural phenomena.

One example of a naïve idea common to children is that trees are not plants. Children may believe this because trees have a trunk, which is more solid than what grasses, shrubs, and other common plants are supported by. As teachers or parents, we must try to help young scientists see that trees have all of the major structural attributes that all other plants have: Trees have roots, stems, and leaves and use sunlight and water to build their structure.

Another major preconception is believing that seeds are fruits. A seed and a piece of fruit have many technical differences. For example, the fruit and the seed develop from different parts of a fertilized cell. In general, fruits *contain* seeds, and sometimes (as in the case of aggregate fruits such as raspberries) fruits contain *many* seeds. For example, the floating dandelion and milkweed fruits contain the little "parachute" as well as the stalk that attaches to the seed, which is an example of a fruit. Thinking about these differences and dissecting fruit can generate a lot of discussion during a hands-on exploration.

As you look at various flowers, children will notice that the carpel is often longer than the pistil. This difference in length helps prevent self-pollination because the tip is above the pollen-bearing pistils. If the tip were below the pistils, gravity could cause pollen to drop on the carpel, thus causing self-pollination. Some plants do self-pollinate regularly, such as tomatoes, dandelions, certain orchids, peas, and peanuts. Self-pollination is a bit of a problem for a plant species, because (a) it eliminates the likelihood of variation in plants, and therefore adaptation to varying ecosystem changes, and (b) it could decrease the vigor of the resulting population. Self-pollination is, however, a means of propagation for plants that are less likely to be visited by their usual pollinators because of location or climate. It is important to realize that the main goal of any living thing is the production of another generation of its kind. However, as you go around closely examining flowers with children, you will find that a multitude of different pollination strategies are fascinating to explore, including those involving factors such as timing (i.e., the pistils and the carpels come out before or after one another).

Here is a quick explanation of germination. Seeds need water to germinate because water gets the hormones working so the food stored in the seed can be used. The first structure that emerges is the primitive root (*radicle*) so that the seed can be anchored in the soil and begin

to transport water. Next, the primitive stem (*epicotyl*) emerges from the soil and pulls up the *plumule*, which has the young leaves (see the diagram on pp. 26–27). These leaves eventually begin to oversee the nutrition of the plant through photosynthesis. It may be interesting to note that no matter which way the seed is planted, the radicle always grows down *toward* the center of the Earth, and the epicotyl grows up *away* from the surface of the Earth.

This book can be a launching point for children's investigation activities. Help your student or child ask, "What would happen if ..." kinds of questions. For example, question 6 on the "Activities" page (p. 32) asks what would happen to a plant if the pistil were cut off. The *Next Generation Science Standards* (NGSS Leads States 2013) recommend that children have an opportunity to dig deeper into the topics they study and use crosscutting concepts that are appropriate for science, engineering, and technology. For example, in the study of flowers and fruits, crosscutting concepts might include looking for patterns or considering how the form of a floral part might relate to its function. Children studying science should also develop skills in planning and carrying out investigations.

The most important message of this book is that plants have special parts that help them reproduce. As mentioned earlier, the nature of any living thing is to focus on the reproduction of its species. Without this reproduction, a species can become extinct. Learning about flowers and fruits is a great way to introduce children to the larger issues of reproduction and extinction and to the joy of observing and uncovering everyday science phenomena.

Reference

NGSS Lead States. 2013. *Next Generation Science Standards: For states, by states.* Washington, DC: National Academies Press. *www. nextgenscience.org/next-generation-science-standards.*